Email Marketing: The Power of Your Inbox

Index:

Conclusion: Maximizing Return on Investment in Email Marketing

Introduction: The Renaissance of Email Marketing

• The Resilience of Email in the Digital Landscape

In the digital age we live in, characterized by constant evolution and innovation, email may seem like a relic of the past. Yet, against all odds, not only has email withstood the test of time, but it has also maintained a central position in the digital marketing landscape. This resilience is the result of a unique combination of reliability, versatility, and adaptability.

Let's start with a fundamental fact: despite the emergence of numerous new communication channels, email remains one of the most widely used forms of communication worldwide. Every day, billions of emails are sent and received, both for personal and professional purposes. This means that an individual's email inbox remains a fundamental and indispensable point of contact, a place that almost everyone visits at least once a day.

Moreover, email offers a level of professionalism and formality that other communication channels often do not achieve. A well-written and well-designed email can create a deep and meaningful interaction between the sender and the recipient, allowing for the building of strong and long-lasting relationships.

But the true strength of email, the one that has allowed it to survive over time, is its incredible adaptability. Email has evolved alongside the digital world, adapting to new technologies and trends. From desktop to mobile, from HTML to responsive design, email has continued to reinvent itself to remain relevant and effective.

In this context, email marketing has emerged as one of the most powerful tools at the disposal of marketers. Thanks to its ability to reach users directly, personalize messages, and track interactions precisely, email marketing offers unique opportunities for engagement and conversion. Not surprisingly, even in 2023, email marketing continues to deliver one of the best returns on investment among all forms of digital marketing.

So, welcome to the renaissance of email marketing. In a world where user attention is increasingly fragmented and hard to capture, email offers a direct and personal way to reach your customers. Are you ready to discover how to make the most of this opportunity?

- **Why Email Marketing Still Matters**

In an era where new digital communication channels emerge daily, one might be tempted to question the relevance of email marketing. However, despite multiple innovations in the field of digital marketing, email marketing retains a position of undisputed importance. You might be wondering why. It's because email marketing is a strategy capable of offering tangible value, a significant return on investment, and a direct connection with your customers.

First and foremost, email marketing provides a direct means of reaching your audience. Unlike social media, where your message must fight to stand out in a sea of content, email goes straight into the recipient's inbox. This means that it's much more likely that your message will be seen, read, and, hopefully, acted upon.

Furthermore, email marketing allows for unprecedented personalization. You can segment your email list based on a myriad of criteria, including age, geographic location, past purchasing behavior, and much more. This means you can send targeted messages that directly address the needs and interests of the recipient, greatly increasing the likelihood of conversion.

Then there's the matter of ROI, return on investment. Email marketing is known for providing one of the highest ROIs of any digital marketing tactic. According to various studies, for every euro spent on email marketing, businesses can expect to see an average return of approximately 38 euros. It's no wonder that email marketing is such a critical component of the marketing mix for so many companies.

Finally, let's not forget the power of email in building and maintaining customer relationships. Email offers a channel for regular and meaningful interactions with your customers, allowing you to build trust and loyalty over time.

This not only helps you retain your current customers but can also turn them into brand ambassadors, ready to spread the word about your business to their friends and family.

In conclusion, while marketing tactics may come and go, email marketing remains a solid and reliable pillar in the digital landscape. It offers a direct and personalized means to connect with your customers, provides an impressive ROI, and helps build lasting relationships. In a constantly changing world, email marketing offers the certainty and stability that every marketer and every business desires.

Chapter 1: Building an Effective Mailing List

1.1 Understanding Your Target Audience

Creating an effective mailing list begins with a fundamental step: a clear understanding of your target audience. This understanding serves as the cornerstone upon which you build all your email marketing strategies. A careful analysis of your target audience not only informs the type of content you should create but also influences when and how you should send your emails.

Start with the most basic question: who are your customers? It's not just about identifying basic demographic data like age, gender, and geographic location. You need to dig deeper. What do they do for a living? What are their interests? What problems are they trying to solve? What motivates them to take action? This deep understanding will enable you to create email marketing messages that resonate with your audience on a personal and meaningful level.

This requires a concerted effort to collect and analyze data. You can use tools like surveys, questionnaires, and interviews to gain direct insight into your audience's needs and desires. At the same time, you should seek to leverage behavioral data such as website interactions, purchase data, and previous email interactions.

But understanding your target audience doesn't stop there. You also need to understand how they prefer to receive communications. What is their email usage behavior? When do they open emails? Do they read emails on desktop or mobile devices? Do they prefer short and direct messages, or do they prefer detailed and in-depth content?

These are all important questions to answer as you strive to understand your target audience. The answers to these questions will enable you to build a mailing list that not only reaches your audience but also speaks directly to their needs, interests, and behaviors. In other words, an effective mailing list.

Email marketing is not a numbers game where the one with the longest list wins. It's a game of relevance and building valuable relationships. And it all starts with understanding your target audience.

Once you have a solid understanding of your audience, the next step is figuring out how to attract them to your mailing list. Now that you know their interests, needs, and the type of content that would resonate with them, you need to formulate a strategy to present them with an offer they can't refuse.

A key element at this stage is the creation of a strong "lead magnet," a high-value offer that website visitors will receive in exchange for subscribing to your mailing list. This could be a special report, a free eBook, an exclusive discount, or any other content or offer that would be of great interest to your target audience.

However, your lead magnet must be closely related to the products or services you offer. If your business is about selling fitness products, an eBook on "how to get sculpted abs" would be an appropriate lead magnet. On the other hand, a special report on "how to grow succulent plants" might not have the same impact, even if it's of high value on its own.

The key lies in the tight connection between your lead magnet and what your business has to offer. This not only helps ensure that people who subscribe to your mailing list are interested in what you do but also serves as a first step toward converting these subscribers into customers.

Throughout this process, it's essential to respect the privacy and preferences of your subscribers. They must have full control over what they receive from you and when they receive it. There should always be a simple and clear way to unsubscribe from your mailing list. Not only is it the right thing to do, but it also helps maintain the quality of your mailing list, ensuring that the people who remain are genuinely interested in what you have to say.

Remember, an effective mailing list isn't built in a day. It takes time, effort, and continuous commitment to understand and serve your audience. But with the right strategy in place, email marketing can become one of the most powerful marketing tools at your disposal.

1.2 Managing Your Mailing List: Cleaning and Segmentation

Having a large and extensive mailing list is undoubtedly an advantage, but what truly makes a difference in the world of email marketing is the quality of this list. A quality contact list is an active, interested, and engaged list in the content you send. That's why it's essential to dedicate time and energy to managing your mailing list, with particular attention to cleaning and segmentation.

List cleaning is a process that involves the removal of invalid, inactive, or unresponsive email addresses. This is a crucial step in maintaining your reputation as a sender and ensuring that your emails actually reach your recipients' inboxes. It may seem counterproductive to remove contacts from your list, but sending emails to addresses that no longer exist or that don't interact with your content can harm your deliverability and the overall effectiveness of your email campaigns.

Another key aspect of mailing list management is segmentation. Not all your subscribers will be interested in everything you have to say or offer. List segmentation allows you to divide your subscribers into specific groups based on various criteria such as behavior, preferences, geographic location, purchase history, and much more. This enables you to personalize your communications to make them as relevant and engaging as possible for each segment.

For example, you might have a segment of customers who have previously purchased from you. For this group, you could create email campaigns that thank them for their support, offer complementary products or services, or request feedback on their purchases.

Another segment might consist of people who have subscribed to your mailing list but haven't made a purchase yet. For these subscribers, you could send emails providing detailed information about your products or services, customer satisfaction testimonials, or special offers to encourage their first purchase.

The goal of email marketing is not just to reach as many people as possible but to engage and create value for the right people, those who are genuinely interested in what you do. List cleaning and segmentation are two powerful tools at your disposal to achieve this goal.

Having recognized the importance of cleaning and segmenting your email list, it's time to delve into techniques and strategies for managing these processes efficiently and effectively. This is where technology and digital marketing tools come into play, simplifying the management of your mailing list and allowing you to focus on what truly matters: building lasting relationships with your customers.

Let's begin by discussing list cleaning. There are various tools available in the market that help you identify and remove inactive or invalid email addresses from your list. These tools can perform regular checks on your list, ensuring it is always up-to-date and clean. Additionally, it's good practice to manually remove subscribers who haven't opened or clicked on your emails for an extended period. This not only maintains your sender reputation but also ensures that you are dedicating your resources to people genuinely interested in your content.

Regarding list segmentation, most email marketing services offer options to segment your subscribers based on various criteria. You can create segments based on subscriber behavior, such as the pages they've visited on your website or the products they've purchased. Other segmentation criteria may include age, gender, geographic location, education level, and many more.

It's important to note that segmentation is not a one-time activity but an ongoing process. As your business grows and changes, you may discover new segmentation opportunities you hadn't considered before. Furthermore, with evolving customer needs and preferences, the segments you've created may need to be reviewed and updated.

A final piece of advice: don't hesitate to experiment and test different list cleaning and segmentation techniques. Every company and every email list are unique, so what works for one business may not work for another. Don't be afraid to try new things and learn from your mistakes. Ultimately, the goal is to create an email list that enables you to achieve your business objectives, whatever they may be.

- **Respecting Privacy and Mailing List Regulations**

In an era dominated by data privacy scandals and growing distrust of companies that do not respect their customers' privacy, it is more important than ever to ensure that your email marketing practices align with current regulations. Responsible mailing list management is not only a legal matter but can also help build your audience's trust and enhance your reputation.

Beyond mere compliance with regulations, respecting recipient privacy can actually improve the effectiveness of your email marketing campaigns. When users feel respected and valued, they are more likely to engage with your messages and respond positively to your offers. This creates a virtuous cycle of trust and engagement that can lead to significant results for your business.

First and foremost, it's essential to understand that sending emails to individuals without their explicit consent is not only unethical but can also result in severe legal penalties. Several countries have introduced strict laws to protect consumers from spam and unwanted communications. For example, the European Union's General Data Protection Regulation (GDPR) and the United States' CAN-SPAM Act establish clear rules regarding consent, personal data management, and the option for recipients to easily unsubscribe from mailing lists.

To comply with these regulations, it's crucial to implement clear procedures for obtaining user consent. Consent should be informed, specific, and freely given. This means you must clearly explain why you are collecting email addresses, how they will be used, and that users can revoke their consent at any time.

This is why it's important to take a proactive approach to protect your subscribers' privacy. Ensure that your signup forms are clear and transparent, that your messages always include prominent and easy-to-use unsubscribe options, and that you strictly respect your subscribers' choices. You should never try to circumvent these regulations or "trick" subscribers into staying on your list. Such tactics can harm your reputation and ultimately lead to fewer interactions and conversions.

In other words, you should always provide a simple and clear mechanism for users who wish to unsubscribe from your list. This is not only a legal requirement but also good business practice. A customer who has a good experience unsubscribing from your list is more likely to return in the future compared to one who feels trapped in an endless stream of unwanted emails.

It's equally important to handle the personal data you collect with care. You must ensure that it is adequately protected and used only for the purposes for which it was collected. This includes limiting access to data, using appropriate security measures, and taking responsibility in case of data breaches.

In conclusion, in an increasingly privacy-conscious digital world, compliance with mailing list regulations is not only a legal obligation but also a smart marketing strategy. Responsible management of mailing lists is a crucial component of a successful email marketing strategy.

By respecting privacy regulations and paying attention to the needs and concerns of your users, you can build lasting and trustful relationships with your mailing list audience in an ethical and effective manner. Furthermore, remember that privacy is not only about legal compliance but also a fundamental aspect of the user experience. A user who feels secure sharing their data with you is a user who trusts you, and trust is the foundation of any long-lasting customer relationship.

Capitolo 2: Creating Email Campaigns that Convert

2.1 The Language of Marketing Emails: Tone and Style

The language we choose for our marketing emails is a critical element in determining how our recipients perceive our brand and, ultimately, the success of our campaigns. The tone and style in which we communicate can either create a sense of closeness and affinity or push our readers away. But what does it really mean to talk about the "tone" and "style" of marketing emails?

The tone of an email is the emotional atmosphere we convey through our words. It's the written equivalent of how our voice would sound if we were speaking in person. A tone can be formal or informal, professional or friendly, serious or playful, depending on our brand's identity and our audience's expectations. It's essential to remember that the tone we choose must be consistent with the message we're trying to convey and the context we're operating in. For example, a youthful and informal tone might work well for a streetwear fashion brand but may not be equally effective for a financial consulting firm.

Style, on the other hand, refers to the choice of words, sentence structure, punctuation, and formatting. It's how we put words together to create our messages. Good writing style is one that manages to be clear and persuasive, regardless of the complexity of the message. However, like tone, style must also be tailored to our audience. We must be able to speak their language, use their terms, and respect their conventions.

The language of marketing emails, therefore, is not just a matter of grammar or word choice. It's a way to build a connection with our recipients, to make them feel understood and appreciated. It's a way to show them that we understand their needs and desires and that we have the right solution for them. And, most importantly, it's a way to convey the personality and values of our brand, so that recipients not only read our emails but also connect with us on a deeper level.

In conclusion, the choice of language in marketing emails is a fundamental aspect of our strategy. It's not just about "saying the right things" but about "saying them in the right way." The right way is the one that resonates with our audience, reflects our brand identity, and allows us to create an authentic and lasting connection.

2.2 The Power of the Subject Line: How to Capture Attention

The email subject, or "subject line," represents the recipient's first impression of your message. It can be crucial in deciding whether the email will be opened or relegated to the oblivion of the inbox. A compelling subject can be the key element that allows your message to stand out in the sea of unread emails.

The power of the email subject lies in its primary task: capturing the recipient's attention. The goal is to create an immediate impact, stimulate curiosity or a need, so as to encourage the recipient to click and open the email. But how can you do this in practice?

Firstly, the subject should be concise and to the point. Studies show that the ideal length of an email subject is about 30-50 characters. Keep in mind that many people check their email on mobile devices, where overly long subjects can be cut off.

Secondly, the subject should be relevant and clear. The recipient should immediately understand what the email is about. A cryptic or misleading subject can lead to the email being ignored, or worse, marked as spam.

Thirdly, the subject should be interesting. This might mean using lively language, asking a provocative question, presenting an irresistible offer, or addressing an issue relevant to the recipient.

Additionally, the subject can benefit from the use of relevant keywords. This not only helps the recipient quickly understand the email's content but can also improve email deliverability by avoiding spam filters.

Finally, consider using personalization in the email subject, such as the recipient's name. This can increase the open rate, as people tend to respond positively when they see their name.

Creating an Effective Email Subject is both an art and a science. It requires a good understanding of your audience, a pinch of creativity, and some testing and measurement. But when done correctly, it can transform email marketing from a simple communication method into a powerful conversion tool. Remember, your email subject is the key that opens the door to a conversation with your recipient. Make sure it's a well-crafted key.

2.3 Creating an Engaging Message: Email Body and Call-to-Action

Once the recipient has opened the email, motivated by a compelling subject, the body of the message takes center stage. The email content must align with what was promised in the subject, keeping the recipient's attention alive and guiding them toward the desired action. This is the crucial point in creating an engaging message.

The first part of the email body should focus on confirming and expanding upon the topic introduced in the subject. Here, you must promptly answer the recipient's question, "What's in it for me?" Make it immediately clear the value or benefit that could result from reading the email, whether it's useful knowledge, a special offer, or an important update.

The tone and style of the email body should reflect your brand and the audience you are addressing. If your brand is formal and professional, your email language should be the same. If, on the other hand, your brand is more friendly and informal, then your email language should reflect this atmosphere.

Incorporate a balanced mix of text, images, and white space in the email body. This helps break up the content and makes it more readable. Visual elements can be extremely powerful in conveying a message quickly and in evoking an emotion or action.

At the end of the email, after providing value and creating a sense of urgency or desire, comes the call-to-action (CTA). This is the moment when you ask the recipient to take a step forward: visit your website, purchase a product, register for an event, respond to the email, and so on. The CTA should be short, clear, and captivating. It should precisely indicate what the recipient should do and what benefits they will receive. The design of the CTA may vary, but it often consists of a colored button or a bold link.

The email body and the CTA are critical elements for the success of an email campaign. Every word, image, and formatting should be carefully chosen and designed with the aim of creating an engaging and smooth experience for the recipient. At the same time, you should monitor and test the performance of your emails so that you can refine and improve your messages over time. Effective email marketing is a continuous learning process, where each new campaign builds on the lessons learned from previous ones.

2.4 Email Design: Effective Templates and Layouts

When it comes to email campaigns, one of the crucial aspects to pay attention to is the design of the template and the layout of the email. This is because the visual appearance of the email not only helps capture the recipient's attention but also reflects your brand, its personality, and its values. Effective email design is one that combines aesthetics and functionality, providing a visually pleasing experience while guiding the recipient towards the desired action.

The email template is the visual framework of your message. It should be chosen and designed to reflect your brand's identity and be easily recognizable. Colors, fonts, images, logos, and other graphic elements should be consistent with your brand and other communications you send. A good template allows you to vary the content while maintaining a consistent basic structure and design.

The email layout, on the other hand, is the organization of content within the template. How you position text, images, links, and the call-to-action can have a significant impact on the email's readability and its ability to guide the recipient to take action. A good layout is intuitive and linear, guiding the recipient's gaze through the various elements of the email in a logical and engaging manner.

Some principles to keep in mind in designing the layout include:

1. Visual Hierarchy: Give more prominence to the most important elements, using size, colors, images, or white space to guide the recipient's attention.

2. Balance: Create a balance between text and images, avoiding overloading the email with too many elements or leaving too much white space.

3. Consistency: Use consistent styles, colors, and fonts throughout the email to create a smooth and harmonious experience.

4. Clarity: Ensure that your call-to-action is clear and highly visible, and that the path to follow is intuitive.

5. Responsiveness: Remember that many people will read the email on their mobile devices, so your design should be responsive and adapt to different screen sizes.

In summary, email design is an essential aspect of email marketing. A well-designed template and an effective layout can not only enhance the aesthetics of your emails but also increase the open rate, click-through rate, and ultimately the return on investment of your email campaigns. Always remember to test and optimize your designs to find what works best for your audience and your goals.

2.5 The Importance of Mobile Optimization

In today's digital landscape, mobile optimization is no longer an option but an essential requirement. According to the latest statistics, more than 60% of email users open their emails on a mobile device. Our world has become "mobile-first," and email marketing strategies must adapt to this change.

An email that is not optimized for mobile devices can be difficult to read, with text that is too small, links too close together, oversized images that go off the screen, or layouts that simply don't fit well on smaller screens. These issues can frustrate recipients, decrease their user experience, and reduce the effectiveness of your email campaigns.

On the contrary, a mobile-optimized email can create a pleasant and seamless user experience, increase the open and click-through rates, and lead to greater engagement and conversion. Mobile-optimized emails display correctly on any device, adapt to screen sizes, are easy to read and navigate, and highlight the most important information and call-to-action elements.

To achieve this, there are several strategies you can adopt. For example, you can use responsive design, which automatically adapts to screen sizes. You can keep your layout simple and clean, avoiding overloading the email with too many elements. You can use appropriately sized text that is easy to read on a small screen. You can ensure that your links and buttons are large enough and well-spaced to be easily clickable. Finally, you can test your emails on different devices and platforms to ensure they display correctly.

Mobile optimization is, therefore, an essential element of email marketing in today's digital world. Ignoring this trend means risking losing a significant portion of your audience and reducing the effectiveness of your email campaigns.
On the contrary, by adopting a "mobile-first" strategy, you can reach and engage your audience where they truly are: on their mobile devices. In an increasingly mobile world, this can make the difference between a successful email campaign and one that fails to achieve its goals.

Chapter 3: A/B Testing in Email Marketing

3.1 Introduction to A/B Testing

A/B testing is a fundamental pillar in the field of email marketing, an indispensable tool that allows you to make data-driven decisions rather than relying on mere instinct or assumptions. Also known as split testing, A/B testing is an experimental method that enables you to compare two versions of the same email to determine which one performs better.

The essence of A/B testing is simple: you take an element of the email that you want to test, such as the subject line, design, call-to-action, or send time, create two different versions of that element (Version A and Version B), then send these two versions to two similar groups of your audience and monitor the results to see which version had better performance. This provides you with a data-based understanding of what works and what doesn't with your audience, allowing you to optimize your future email campaigns.

However, the strength of A/B testing lies not only in its simplicity but also in its versatility and power. No matter how much experience or knowledge you have in the field of email marketing, there is no "one-size-fits-all" approach that works for all audiences in every situation. What works for one company or industry may not work for another. What worked yesterday may not work today. That's why A/B testing is so valuable: it gives you the flexibility and the ability to adapt your email marketing strategies to the evolving needs, behaviors, and preferences of your audience.

Furthermore, A/B testing is not a one-time event but a continuous process of learning and improvement. With each test you conduct, you accumulate new data and insights that you can use to further refine your email campaigns. And over time, even small improvements can add up to a significant impact on your conversion rate, ROI, and the overall success of your email marketing strategies.

A/B Testing is, therefore, a powerful and versatile tool that can transform your approach to email marketing. In the following pages, we will delve into how to implement A/B testing in your email campaigns, how to choose the variables to test, how to interpret the results, and how to use these insights to optimize your future campaigns. So, get ready to step into the exciting and informative world of A/B testing in email marketing.

3.2 Creating an A/B Test: Selecting Variables and Setting up the Test

Creating an A/B test begins with selecting variables and setting up the test, a process that requires both a strategic vision and careful attention to detail.

A variable, in the context of A/B testing, is the specific element of the email you want to put to the test. It could be the email subject line, design, message content, call-to-action, sending time, or any other element you believe may impact your email's performance. The key is to choose a variable that is relevant to your goal. For example, if you're aiming to increase your email open rate, you may want to test different versions of the email subject line.

Once the variable is chosen, the next step is setting up the test. This means creating two different versions of the email - Version A and Version B - that differ only in the variable you've chosen to test. This uniformity is crucial to ensure that any performance difference between the two versions can be attributed to the variable in question and not to other factors.

However, setting up the test is not just about creating Versions A and B of the email. It also means deciding to whom you will send these versions and how you will measure the results. Typically, you'll want to send Version A and Version B to two similar but distinct segments of your audience so that you can make a fair comparison between the two. And you'll need a system in place to monitor and record relevant data, such as the open rate, click-through rate, conversion rate, or any other metrics relevant to your goal.

Remember, A/B testing is not a shot in the dark. It's a scientific exercise that requires critical thinking, careful planning, and rigorous data analysis. But when executed correctly, it can provide valuable insights that help you optimize your email campaigns, improve your communication with your audience, and ultimately drive your business towards success. So, take the time to set up your A/B tests carefully, and be prepared to discover the transformative power of this potent email marketing practice.

3.3 Analyzing the Results: Interpreting the Data

The crucial next step after conducting an A/B test is the analysis of results. This involves a thorough interpretation of the data collected to understand the significance of what has emerged from the comparison between Version A and Version B of your emails.

Let's start from the beginning: when we look at the results of an A/B test, the main goal is to determine which version performed better in terms of the objective we are trying to achieve.

But, most importantly, we need to understand if the differences in the results between the two versions are statistically significant or if they can be simply attributed to chance.

For example, let's imagine we've conducted an A/B test on email subject lines with the goal of increasing the open rate. Version A uses a declarative subject line, while Version B uses a question. After sending the emails, we record an open rate of 20% for Version A and 22% for Version B. At first glance, Version B seems to have slightly better performance. But the question is: is this difference statistically significant?

Here's where statistical tests like the Student's t-test or chi-squared test come into play, allowing us to calculate the p-value - the probability that the observed differences are due to chance. If the p-value is lower than a certain threshold level, for example, 0.05, we can reject the hypothesis that the differences are due to chance and conclude that Version B is indeed superior.

But data interpretation isn't just about determining which version is better. It's also an opportunity to gain insights into your audience and their interaction with your emails. For example, in the case of the subject line test, if you find that Version B - the one with the question - performed better, it might indicate that your audience responds better to emails that arouse curiosity or create a sense of mystery.

Analyzing the results is a crucial step in the A/B testing process, a moment where raw numbers are transformed into valuable insights. With careful data interpretation, you can optimize your emails and, as a result, improve your connection with your audience.

3.4 Optimizing Campaigns Based on Test Results

When we talk about optimizing email campaigns based on the results of A/B tests, we're referring to a two-phase process: result interpretation and implementation of changes.

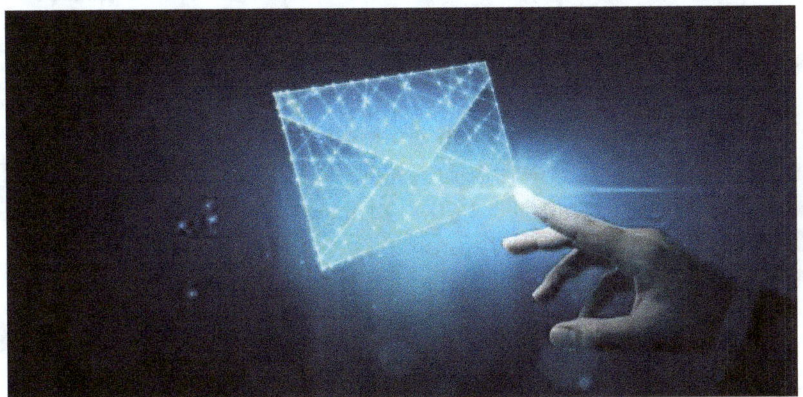

Result interpretation, as discussed in the previous section, involves turning raw test result numbers into meaningful insights. This phase allows us to understand which version of the emails performed better and why.

Once interpretation is completed, we move on to the second phase: implementing changes. Here, the goal is to use the insights gained to improve future email campaigns.

To do this, we need to be prepared to question and revise any aspect of our campaign. If the test showed that a certain subject line leads to a higher open rate, we should consider using similar subject lines in future emails. If we've discovered that recipients respond better to emails sent at a specific time of day, we should adjust the scheduling of our emails accordingly.

In some cases, changes can be quite substantial, involving a complete overhaul of the email design or message tone. In others, only minor adjustments may be needed. But regardless of the scope of the changes, the goal remains the same: to continuously improve the performance of our email campaigns.

However, it's important to remember that optimization is an ongoing process. Even after making changes based on the results of an A/B test, it's a good practice to continue testing and refining. Audience preferences can change over time, and what works today may not work tomorrow. Through constant testing and optimization, we can keep our email campaigns in step with these changes and continue to reach, and even surpass, our marketing goals.

CAMPAIGN
MESSAGE
BENCHMARK
MESSAGE
E-MAIL
MARKETING
RESEARCH
CONTENT
TARGET

Chapter 4: Automation and Personalization in Email

4.1 The Benefits of Email Marketing Automation

Email marketing automation, one of the most powerful features available to digital marketers, has revolutionized how businesses connect and engage with their customers. No longer constrained by the inevitable barrier of time, marketers can now plan, develop, and send highly targeted email marketing campaigns in a timely and relevant manner, taking customer engagement to an entirely new level.

One of the key benefits of email marketing automation is efficiency. Tasks that once required hours of manual work, such as sending welcome emails to new subscribers or communicating special offers to loyal customers, can now be automated, freeing up valuable time to focus on more strategic aspects of email marketing. This also means greater consistency and reliability in customer communications, as human errors are minimized.

But automation doesn't just bring efficiency; it also brings personalization. With email marketing automation, businesses can leverage customer data to create personalized messages that cater to their specific needs and interests.

For example, a customer who has just purchased a pair of shoes from an online clothing store might receive an automated email with recommendations for other items they might like based on their past purchases. This level of personalization can lead to greater customer engagement and loyalty, as each email becomes a tailored experience rather than a generic promotional message.

Email marketing automation can also contribute to improving customer knowledge, as it allows for the collection of detailed customer behavior data. This data can be used to further refine email campaigns and inform marketing decisions in other areas.

The benefits of email marketing automation are manifold: it increases efficiency, enables greater personalization, enhances customer knowledge, and can lead to higher customer engagement. It's an indispensable tool for any business looking to maximize the power of email marketing.

4.2 Creating Automated Email Journeys: From Welcome to Abandoned Cart

Creating automated email journeys is both an art and a science that blends into the wonderful world of Email Marketing. It involves setting in motion a series of email communications that respond to customer actions and behaviors, guiding them through a path that goes from welcoming to loyalty, encompassing all the intermediate stages of the customer lifecycle.

Let's start from the beginning: the welcome email. This is often the first direct contact a customer has with your brand after subscribing to your mailing list. It's the opportunity to introduce yourself, set expectations about what the customer can expect from you, and most importantly, start building a relationship. An automated email journey can begin with a simple welcome email, followed by a series of communications that introduce the customer to your brand and your products or services.

But automation doesn't stop there. After the introduction, there are many other stages in the customer lifecycle where automated email can play a crucial role. For instance, you could set up an email journey for customers who have shown interest in a particular product or service, providing additional information or even special offers to encourage a purchase.

Then, there's the purchase experience. Here, automated email can help manage and enhance the customer journey, from order to delivery. For example, you could send an automatic email to confirm the order, another to notify shipping, and a third to request feedback after delivery.

Last but certainly not least, there's the phenomenon of abandoned carts. It's a common issue in the world of e-commerce: a customer adds a product to the cart but doesn't complete the purchase. This is where an automated email journey can make a difference. An automatic email can be sent after a certain period of inactivity, reminding the customer of the items left in the cart and encouraging them to complete the purchase, perhaps with a special offer or discount.

In summary, creating automated email journeys means building a series of email communications that guide the customer along their path, responding to their actions and behaviors promptly and relevantly. It's a powerful way to enhance the customer experience, increase conversions, and ultimately build stronger relationships with your customers.

4.3 The Power of Personalization: From Name to Dynamic Content

We are in the heart of the 21st century, and the era of generic emails has passed. Now, email marketing is all about personalization. But what exactly is personalization, and why is it so powerful? Personalization in email marketing is not just a way to make your communications more attractive and engaging; it's a way to show your customers that you know them, understand their needs, and are ready to meet them.

Let's start with the simplest but no less effective aspect of personalization: using the recipient's name. Including the recipient's name in the email subject or body can work wonders for the open and click-through rates. It's a small touch that adds a level of personalization and makes the email much more appealing. But remember, personalization must be accurate. An error in the recipient's name can have the opposite effect, creating a sense of distance and impersonality.

In addition to using the name, personalization can be taken to the next level through the use of dynamic content. Dynamic content is parts of the email that change based on the information you have about the recipient. This can include demographic information such as age or geographic location, or behavioral information like past purchases or website browsing.

For example, you could send an email with a special offer on a product the recipient viewed on your website, or you could send an email with product recommendations based on past purchases. You could also personalize the email based on the recipient's geographic location, showing relevant offers or events in their area.

This level of personalization requires a good amount of data and analysis, but it can lead to surprising results. Personalized emails tend to have higher open and click-through rates and can help build stronger relationships with customers. After all, who doesn't appreciate a personalized experience that caters to their tastes and needs?

In conclusion, personalization is a powerful tool in email marketing. From using the recipient's name to dynamic content, every level of personalization can contribute to improving the effectiveness of your emails and building stronger relationships with your customers. So, do not underestimate the power of personalization; it can make the difference between an email that gets opened and read and one that gets ignored.

Chapter 5: Email Campaign Performance Analysis

5.1 KPIs in Email Marketing: Open Rate, Click-Through Rate, Conversions

In the world of marketing, performance measurement is an essential element for evaluating the effectiveness of your strategies. Without measuring results, you risk sailing blindly, unable to understand if the course you've taken is the right one or if a change of direction is necessary. Email marketing is no exception to this rule, and there are numerous metrics, or Key Performance Indicators (KPIs), that can help you understand how your campaigns are performing.

Let's start with the open rate, one of the most fundamental KPIs in email marketing. But before delving into the heart of the discussion, it's crucial to understand what the open rate actually represents.

In the context of email marketing, this metric calculates the percentage of recipients who have opened the email you sent compared to the total number of emails sent. Imagine you sent 1000 emails, and you got 200 opens. Your open rate, in this case, would be 20%.

The open rate is one of the primary indicators of your email marketing campaign's performance. It's the first interaction that the user has with your email: to open or ignore the message. If people don't open your emails, they won't have the opportunity to interact with your content, links, or offers.

A high open rate is generally a positive signal. It means that the subject line of your email, along with the sender, is effectively capturing the recipient's attention and piquing their curiosity, prompting them to open the message. It's a preview of the value you're offering inside the email, a promise of utility or interest that has attracted the recipient.

But if you notice a low open rate, it could be a warning sign indicating a problem. This might mean that your subject lines aren't engaging enough, that your recipient list isn't well-segmented, or that you're sending emails at suboptimal times. If your open rate falls short of expectations, you should consider revising and optimizing your subject line and sending strategy.

Remember, the subject line of your email is the first contact your recipient has with your message. It's the business card that can determine whether the email will be opened or ignored. An effective subject line should be concise, relevant, and attention-grabbing, stimulating the recipient's curiosity and promising value that will encourage them to open the email.

Overall, the open rate is a crucial indicator of the health of your email marketing campaigns. It's not the only one, nor the most important, but it provides a basic picture of the level of interest your recipients show in your communications. Ignoring it, or worse, underestimating it, could lead to a series of problems and missed opportunities.

Next is the click-through rate (CTR), which measures the percentage of recipients who have clicked on one of the links in the email. The click-through rate, or CTR, answers a fundamental question in the world of email marketing: once recipients have opened your email, are they interested in what you have to say? The CTR measures the percentage of recipients who have clicked on one or more of the links in your email. For example, if 100 people open your email, and 10 of them click on a link, your CTR is 10%.

The CTR is a direct indicator of the effectiveness and relevance of your content. It measures how interested recipients are in what you're offering and how willing they are to engage with your email. If your CTR is high, it means that recipients find your content useful, interesting, and worthy of their attention. They see value in the time they invest in exploring your emails and clicking on the links you provide.

On the other hand, a low CTR can indicate various issues. It might mean that the content of your email is not relevant to the recipients. Or perhaps your email design is confusing, making it difficult for recipients to find and click on your links. It could also suggest that recipients don't see enough value in your content to invest time in exploring it further.

The beauty of the CTR, however, is that it provides direct and immediate feedback on how your recipients are reacting to your content. You can use this information to make adjustments and improve your email marketing strategy.

For example, if you consistently notice a low CTR, you might want to examine your content. Are you providing real value to your recipients? Do your content answer their questions, solve their problems, or entertain them in some way? If they don't, it might be time to reconsider what you're sending.

Similarly, if your CTR is low, it might be time to revisit the design of your emails. Are your links clearly visible and easy to find? Is your design clean and free from distractions that could divert recipients away from your links? Effective email design can make a big difference in your CTR.

The CTR is a fundamental metric in email marketing. It's a direct gauge of your recipients' interest and engagement, and it can provide valuable insights into how to improve your email marketing campaigns.

Last but not least, we have the conversion rate.
The conversion rate is the final stop in the email marketing journey, and many people consider it the most important metric. While the open rate tells you if your email grabs attention, and the CTR tells you if your content interests your recipients, the conversion rate tells you if your email marketing efforts are producing the desired results.

The conversion rate measures the percentage of recipients who, after clicking on a link in your email, have then taken a desired action. This action could be making a purchase, registering for a webinar, filling out a survey, downloading a document, or any other action you have defined as the goal of your email marketing campaign.

For example, if 100 recipients click on a link in your email, and 10 of them make a purchase, your conversion rate is 10%. In other words, you've converted 10% of the visitors into customers.

The conversion rate is crucial because it reflects how effective your emails are in driving recipients to take an action that adds value to your business. If your conversion rate is high, it means that your emails are not only relevant and interesting but also effective in persuading recipients to take action.

However, a low conversion rate shouldn't necessarily be cause for panic. It may simply indicate that there are areas of your email marketing strategy that could be improved. Perhaps your call-to-action isn't compelling enough. Maybe your link leads to a confusing or unattractive landing page. Or perhaps the step you're asking recipients to take is too big or too complicated.

The beauty of the conversion rate is that, like the CTR, it provides direct and tangible feedback on how you're doing. You can use this information to fine-tune and improve your emails, making them more effective over time.

So, the conversion rate is a fundamental metric for any email marketing campaign. It not only reflects the success of your emails in driving action but can also provide valuable insights into how to improve your email marketing strategies in the future.

These are just some of the KPIs that can help you measure the effectiveness of your email marketing campaigns, but they deserved a thorough discussion. Always remember that these metrics should not be evaluated in isolation but within the broader context of your marketing strategy. The open rate, CTR, and conversion rate will provide you with valuable information, but you'll need to interpret them in light of your specific business needs and goals.

5.2 Analysis of Results and Optimization of Future Campaigns

Result analysis is the lighthouse in the tumultuous sea of email marketing. The act of carefully examining numbers, percentages, and trends not only gives us a sense of how a particular campaign performed but can also point the way for future campaigns.

Once you have your KPIs - open rate, CTR, conversion rate - at your fingertips, it's time to enter an analysis phase. And it's not just about looking at the numbers; it's about understanding what these numbers are saying. A low open rate might suggest the need to revisit email subject lines or the timing of sending. A low CTR might indicate the need for a review of email content or layout. A low conversion rate might highlight the need to revise the call-to-action or the landing page that the email link leads to.

This detailed analysis is the key to unlocking the optimization of future campaigns. Every email marketing campaign is a lesson; every result, a teacher. Knowing how to listen, understand, and act based on these lessons can make the difference between a good campaign and a great one.

But optimization is not just a process of correcting mistakes; it's also an opportunity to amplify what's working. If a particular type of email subject line consistently gets a high open rate, it's worth exploring and understanding what makes that subject line so attractive. If a certain type of content generates a high CTR, why not experiment and see if you can incorporate more of it into future campaigns?

Every email marketing campaign is a piece in the mosaic of optimization. Every analysis you do, every lesson you learn, every action you take contributes to building a stronger, more refined, and more effective email marketing strategy.

Analysis of results, therefore, can be said to be not just an endpoint but a starting point. It's the launchpad for optimizing future campaigns, the opportunity to take what you've learned and use it to improve, grow, and, most importantly, convert. Because, in the end, that's the power of email marketing: the ability to reach, engage, and convert recipients effectively and at scale. And analysis and optimization are the tools that allow you to wield that power to the best of your abilities.

5.3 Case Study: Successful Email Marketing Campaigns

In the world of email marketing, success stories can serve as a compass, guiding us through the intricacies of strategies, optimization, and analysis. When we explore these successful case studies, we gain a rare and valuable insight into how email marketing campaigns can achieve their goals and, ultimately, drive business growth.

Imagine, for example, an online clothing retailer. Despite having a large customer database, their email marketing campaign was not generating the desired engagement. After careful analysis of their KPIs, they found that the subject lines of their emails were not engaging enough, leading to a low open rate. In response, they began experimenting with more personalized and action-oriented subject lines, testing different variations through A/B testing. The result? A significant increase in the open rate, a crucial first step towards greater engagement.

But their work didn't stop there. They turned their attention to the click-through rate, examining the layout and content of their emails. Through further testing and optimizations, they improved their CTR by implementing cleaner designs, more relevant content, and stronger calls to action. This led to an increase in traffic to their website, a critical outcome for an e-commerce business.

Finally, they focused on the conversion rate. Analyzing the data, they discovered that many users were leaving the website without completing a purchase. To combat this issue of abandoned carts, they implemented a series of personalized follow-up emails, offering special discounts and reminding customers of items left in their carts. This resulted in a significant increase in the conversion rate and underscored the importance of automation in email marketing.

This case study is just one example of how data analysis, continuous optimization, and a deep understanding of the audience can transform an email marketing campaign. Every campaign has the potential to be a success if we know where to look and how to act. And as this case demonstrates, the key to success lies in being always ready to learn, adapt, and improve.

It doesn't matter where you start; what matters is where you decide to go. With the right combination of strategy, analysis, and action, success is within reach. And when you reach that point, you'll not only have a successful email marketing campaign but also a success story of your own to tell.

Chapter 6: Advanced Email Marketing Strategies

6.1 Using Advanced Techniques: Retargeting, Drip Campaigns, Upselling

Navigating the deeper waters of email marketing, we encounter a series of advanced techniques that can open new doors for your business. Retargeting, drip campaigns, and upselling are some of these strategies, each with the potential to elevate your email campaigns to the next level.

Let's start with retargeting, an art that involves reconnecting with recipients who have already interacted with your brand, such as visiting your website or clicking on a previous email.

In the intricate labyrinth of digital marketing, retargeting emerges as a well-lit path, guiding brands toward closer interaction with their audience. But let's proceed step by step, delving into what retargeting exactly is.

Retargeting is a type of online marketing that allows you to stay in touch with your visitors after they have left your website. Imagine a potential customer visits your site, explores a product or service, but then leaves the page without making a purchase. This is where retargeting comes into play: by using tracking cookies, it enables you to send targeted ads to that specific person, attempting to bring them back to your site to complete the initial action.

The reason why retargeting is so effective lies in human psychology. Familiarity plays a key role in this context. Recipients who have already interacted with your brand have a basic awareness of your products or services. This level of awareness, or familiarity, makes it more likely for these recipients to become loyal customers over time.

A retargeting campaign, therefore, specifically targets these individuals, using personalized emails to establish a direct connection with them. These emails are not generic but carefully crafted to resonate with the recipient, often reminding them of the product or service they had previously explored. Retargeting emails may contain special offers, discounts, or reminders, creating a sense of urgency that encourages the recipient to return to your site and complete the desired action.

In essence, retargeting allows you to reestablish a connection with potential customers who have already shown interest in your offering. Through targeted and personalized communications, you not only regain the recipient's attention on your brand but also create a deeper sense of connection, increasing the likelihood of transforming a mere visitor into a loyal customer. This is the power of retargeting, a potent lever in the world of email marketing.

Now, let's move on to drip campaigns, also known as nurturing campaigns.

In the intricate labyrinth of digital marketing, retargeting emerges as a well-lit path, guiding brands toward closer interaction with their audience. But let's proceed step by step, delving into what retargeting exactly is.

Retargeting is a type of online marketing that allows you to stay in touch with your visitors after they have left your website. Imagine a potential customer visits your site, explores a product or service, but then leaves the page without making a purchase. This is where retargeting comes into play: by using tracking cookies, it enables you to send targeted ads to that specific person, attempting to bring them back to your site to complete the initial action.

The reason why retargeting is so effective lies in human psychology. Familiarity plays a key role in this context.

Recipients who have already interacted with your brand have a basic awareness of your products or services. This level of awareness, or familiarity, makes it more likely for these recipients to become loyal customers over time.

A retargeting campaign, therefore, specifically targets these individuals, using personalized emails to establish a direct connection with them. These emails are not generic but carefully crafted to resonate with the recipient, often reminding them of the product or service they had previously explored. Retargeting emails may contain special offers, discounts, or reminders, creating a sense of urgency that encourages the recipient to return to your site and complete the desired action.

In essence, retargeting allows you to reestablish a connection with potential customers who have already shown interest in your offering. Through targeted and personalized communications, you not only regain the recipient's attention on your brand but also create a deeper sense of connection, increasing the likelihood of transforming a mere visitor into a loyal customer. This is the power of retargeting, a potent lever in the world of email marketing.

Now, let's move on to drip campaigns, also known as nurturing campaigns.

Drip campaigns, or nurturing campaigns, represent a more sophisticated and deliberate approach to email marketing. These campaigns derive their name from the "drip" irrigation technique, which provides water to plants in small, constant amounts over time, just like these campaigns deliver content to recipients gradually and consistently.

Drip campaigns are designed with the goal of guiding the recipient along a predefined path, with each email serving as a piece of a larger mosaic. Each message is carefully crafted to build a story or sequence of events, aiming to keep the recipient engaged and interested. This strategy can be likened to reading a book or watching a TV series, where each chapter or episode builds the plot and stimulates interest in the next one.

A classic example of a drip campaign is the series of welcome emails for new subscribers. Upon signing up, the recipient may receive a welcome email thanking them for choosing your company and introducing the benefits of the subscription. After a few days, another email might arrive, introducing one of your key products or services. A third email might contain testimonials from satisfied customers, and so on. Each email serves a specific purpose, and together they create a discovery path that leads the recipient to become a loyal customer.

Drip campaigns can also be used to educate recipients about a product or service. For example, you could send a series of emails explaining how to use a product, highlighting its unique features, and addressing common questions. These types of campaigns not only provide tremendous value to recipients but also establish your company as a trusted source of information, strengthening customer trust and loyalty.

The key to creating an effective nurturing campaign lies in balance: each email should provide enough information to be valuable on its own but not so much as to overwhelm the recipient or spoil the sense of anticipation for future emails. After all, the goal of a drip campaign is to keep the recipient engaged and interested throughout the entire journey, bringing them closer to the final conversion.

Lastly, let's talk about upselling, a technique as simple as it is effective.

Upselling is an essential marketing strategy that focuses on encouraging customers to upgrade their current purchase to a higher-value product or service. The beauty of this tactic lies in its simplicity: instead of seeking new customers, you concentrate on those who have already shown trust in your brand by making a purchase.

Think of upselling as a form of consultancy. It's not just about selling a more expensive product; it's about helping the customer understand how a higher-tier product or service could better meet their needs or solve their problems. When done ethically and respectfully, upselling can not only increase the average order value but also enhance customer satisfaction, as it helps them get more value from their purchases.

For instance, consider a customer who has just purchased a new laptop. Instead of letting the interaction end there, you could send an email highlighting the benefits of a premium software package. You could illustrate how access to professional software for graphic design, video editing, or office work could enrich their user experience. Or you could suggest an extended warranty that protects their investment for a longer period.

Upselling is effective only when perceived as a benefit rather than a forced sale. The approach should be customer-focused and based on their needs. Every upselling suggestion should be accompanied by a clear and convincing explanation of how the superior product or service will add value for the customer.

Moreover, it's important to remember that upselling should be done appropriately and in a timely manner. The upselling email should be sent shortly after the purchase, while the customer is still in the excitement of the purchase and has your brand fresh in mind. However, you must always respect the customer's preferences and ensure that any upselling communication is sent in compliance with privacy laws and marketing regulations.

When done correctly, upselling can not only significantly increase the average order value but also improve customer loyalty and satisfaction, creating a deeper and more profitable relationship between the customer and your company.

Upselling is not just a sales strategy; it's a way to continue delivering value to your customers and building lasting relationships.

Each of these advanced strategies requires careful planning, a solid understanding of your audience, and a commitment to continuous optimization. But when leveraged to the fullest, they can elevate your email marketing campaigns to unimaginable heights, turning your inbox into a true growth engine for your business.

6.2 Email and Social Media: An Integrated Strategy

In today's digital age, marketing strategies cannot exist in separate silos. Email marketing and social media, two powerful communication channels, can and should work together to achieve the best results. Why, you might ask? Because integrating email and social media can power up your marketing strategy and amplify your efforts, creating a more engaging and personalized experience for your customers.

Imagine for a moment your customers, scrolling through their favorite social media platforms, encountering an enticing post from your company. They click on the post, are directed to your website, and decide to subscribe to your newsletter to stay updated. From that point on, a sophisticated dance unfolds between email and social media, each playing its unique yet interconnected part in guiding the customer along the conversion funnel.

On one hand, emails can provide more detailed and personalized content, offering your customers valuable information, exclusive promotions, or helpful tips.

This helps build trust and nurture the relationship with your customers, encouraging them to remain engaged and active. At the same time, social media serves as ideal platforms to amplify your messages, reaching a broader audience and encouraging interaction and engagement.

For instance, you could share your newsletter on your social media channels, giving your followers a preview of the valuable content they would receive if they subscribed. Or you could use email to encourage your subscribers to follow your social media accounts, where they can see regular posts that keep them informed and engaged.

Another powerful aspect of integrating email and social media is the ability to use data from both channels to enhance your marketing strategy. Data derived from user behaviors on both channels can provide valuable insights into your customers, helping you better understand their interests, preferences, and behaviors. This, in turn, can enable you to refine your messages, better segment your audience, and deliver a more personalized experience.

Let's take the example of a company that sells home and furniture items, let's call it "HomeScape." HomeScape has a significant following on social media and a well-established email newsletter. They want to launch a new collection of living room furniture and decide to develop an integrated email and social media strategy.

They start with a social media post, an enticing photo of a living room furnished with the new collection's furniture, accompanied by an engaging description that piques the curiosity of their followers. The post includes an invitation to subscribe to the newsletter to receive an exclusive preview of the new collection and a special discount.

Simultaneously, HomeScape sends a newsletter to their existing subscribers, introducing the new collection and offering an exclusive preview. The email includes detailed photos of the new furniture and tips on how to decorate the living room. The special discount and the opportunity to pre-order items from the new collection are also mentioned.

Furthermore, the email encourages recipients to follow HomeScape on social media for additional updates and decorating ideas. At the same time, the social media post encourages followers to subscribe to the newsletter to take advantage of the discount and get an exclusive preview.

With this integrated strategy, HomeScape reaches a broader audience, engages existing and potential customers across multiple platforms, and increases the likelihood of conversion. Moreover, they can track click-through data from emails and social media to understand which platform leads to more sales and further optimize their marketing strategies.

In conclusion, the integration of email and social media is not just a strategic choice; it's a necessary step for businesses looking to thrive in today's digital landscape. When email and social media work in synergy, the sum of their efforts can far exceed their individual parts, creating a communication flow that keeps your customers engaged, informed, and connected with your brand.

6.3 The Future of Email Marketing: Artificial Intelligence and Beyond

When we talk about the future of email marketing, we can't ignore the role of Artificial Intelligence (AI). Nowadays, AI has already begun to transform email marketing, and its role is expected to become even more central over time.

Artificial Intelligence can help us create more personalized and relevant email campaigns. For example, machine learning algorithms can analyze user data, such as past purchase behavior, interactions with previous emails, and website browsing, to determine which types of content will be most relevant to each individual. This means that instead of sending the same email to all subscribers, AI allows us to send highly personalized emails that speak directly to the interests and specific needs of each recipient.

Furthermore, AI can make email marketing more efficient. It can automate processes that would otherwise require a significant amount of time, such as subscriber segmentation or optimizing the timing of sends. Algorithms can analyze data to determine the optimal time to send an email to a particular recipient, thus increasing the chances of the email being opened and read.

But AI is not the only future development in email marketing. We must also consider the growing importance of data and analytics. As we accumulate more and more data about our subscribers, we will have more powerful tools to understand their behaviors and preferences. This will allow us to create increasingly effective email campaigns that not only reach the right audience but also speak directly to their desires and needs.

Finally, we must consider the growing role of privacy and security. Users are increasingly concerned about the protection of their personal data, and we must respect these concerns in our email marketing. This means using transparent opt-in practices, safeguarding subscriber data, and ensuring that our emails are secure and protected.

In conclusion, the future of email marketing is bright and full of opportunities. With the help of Artificial Intelligence, data analysis, and a strong commitment to privacy and security, we can create email campaigns that not only reach our audience but engage and enchant them in increasingly personal and meaningful ways. We look forward to seeing where this future will take us.

EMAIL
MARKETING
@
Enter

Appendix: Glossary of Email Marketing Terms

Email Marketing: A digital marketing strategy that involves sending emails to a list of contacts to promote products, services, or events.

Contact List: A list of email addresses from individuals who have given their consent to receive communications from a company.

Segmentation: A process that divides a contact list into smaller groups, or segments, based on specific characteristics, such as geographic location, buying habits, age, and so on.

Open Rate: This term refers to the percentage of recipients who have opened an email compared to the total number of emails sent.

Click-through Rate (CTR): The percentage of recipients who have clicked on one of the links in the email.

Conversion Rate: This metric measures the percentage of recipients who have taken a desired action, such as making a purchase, registering for an event, or downloading a document, after clicking a link in the email.

Retargeting: This marketing strategy involves sending personalized emails to people who have already interacted with a company in some way, such as visiting its website or clicking on a previous email.

Drip Campaigns: These are automated email campaigns that send a series of messages at scheduled intervals.

Upselling: This marketing technique encourages customers to consider a product or service of higher value than what they have already purchased.

Artificial Intelligence (AI): This term refers to computer systems that can perform tasks that would normally require human intervention, such as learning, decision-making, and problem-solving.

A/B Testing: This marketing technique involves comparing two versions of an email to see which version generates better results.

Bounce Rate: The bounce rate refers to the percentage of sent emails that cannot be delivered.

Call to Action (CTA): A CTA is a prompt to take action that encourages the recipient to take a specific action, such as "Buy Now" or "Sign Up."

Lead: A lead is a potential customer who has shown interest in a company's products or services.

Personalization: This practice involves tailoring the content of emails to meet the specific needs or interests of each recipient.

Whitelist: A whitelist is a list of email addresses or domains that a user has approved to receive emails from.

Email Workflow: An email workflow is a series of automated emails that are sent based on specific triggers or dates.

Behavioral Segmentation: This term refers to the process of segmenting the contact list into groups based on their past behavior, such as previous purchases or email interaction.

CRM (Customer Relationship Management): CRM is a system used to manage and analyze customer interactions and data.

Appendix: Tools and Platforms for Email Marketing

In today's digital landscape, the effectiveness of email marketing is substantially enhanced by using tools and platforms specifically designed to optimize, personalize, and automate your campaigns. These technological solutions can make sending thousands of emails not only possible but also efficient, measurable, and, most importantly, effective in achieving your business goals.

MailChimp: Probably one of the most well-known in the industry, MailChimp offers a comprehensive range of email marketing services, including email creation, automation, data analytics, and contact management. Its intuitive features and customizable templates make it easy even for beginners to create professional email marketing campaigns.

Constant Contact: Besides offering a robust and user-friendly email marketing service, Constant Contact provides a suite of tools for social media marketing, event management, CRM, and more. It has options for email automation, performance tracking, and customization.

GetResponse: GetResponse is another all-in-one solution that provides tools for email marketing, automation, webinars, landing pages, and CRM. It offers advanced features for performance analysis and contact segmentation.

Drip: As the name suggests, Drip excels when it comes to drip campaigns or nurturing email campaigns. It offers powerful marketing automation and deep integration with e-commerce platforms like Shopify.

Sendinblue: This platform is known for its powerful automation capabilities. Sendinblue allows you to create complex email workflows based on customer behavior, making it a great tool for targeted email marketing campaigns.

ActiveCampaign: In addition to offering a complete email marketing service, ActiveCampaign excels in providing sophisticated automation tools. This platform allows you to create and manage a variety of marketing automations, including emails, SMS, chat, and more.

Remember, choosing the right tool for your email marketing needs will depend on several factors, including your specific requirements, budget, level of experience, and the type of integrations you might need. So, while this list provides an excellent starting point, I recommend taking the time to explore each option to see which tool or platform is the best fit for you.

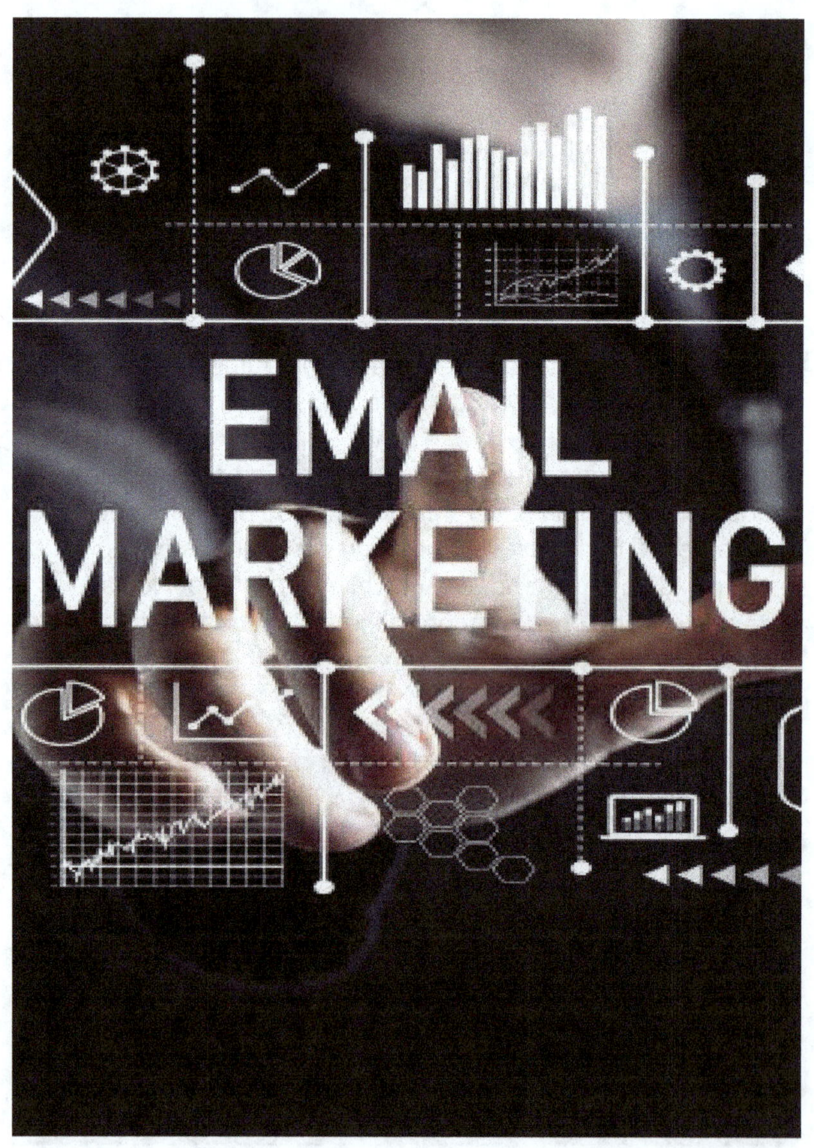
EMAIL
MARKETING

Conclusion: Maximizing Return on Investment in Email Marketing

Together, we've embarked on a fascinating journey, exploring the intricacies of email marketing, unveiling its hidden strategies, and discovering its boundless potential. Along this journey, we've paused to reflect on the most important aspect—the beating heart of every marketing endeavor, the core of every strategy: maximizing the return on investment (ROI) in email marketing. It's time to delve deeper into this crucial topic.

Throughout this book, we've discussed a myriad of strategies, techniques, and ideas—from the art of contact list management to the meticulous analysis of email campaign performance; from advanced strategies to the integration of email and social media. Each of these strategies is not a standalone entity but rather a piece of a much larger mosaic.

Every element is interconnected, and together, they converge toward a common goal: extracting the maximum benefit from your investment in email marketing.

However, ROI in email marketing cannot be simply measured in monetary terms, such as direct profit from sales generated by your email campaigns.

In reality, it includes a range of more intangible but no less important benefits. Among these are the building and solidifying of your brand, improving relationships with your customers, and creating a community of loyal and devoted customers. These elements, while not quantifiable in monetary terms, are equally crucial for the long-term success of your business.

To maximize ROI in email marketing, you need to adopt a holistic approach that goes beyond individual email campaigns. You must understand that every aspect of your email marketing—every email sent, every subject line crafted, every call to action formulated—is part of a larger system that contributes to achieving your business goals. It's precision work where every detail counts and can make a difference.

Also, remember that success in email marketing is not achieved overnight. It's the result of an ongoing process of learning, experimentation, analysis, and optimization. Every email campaign you send, every result you analyze, every feedback you receive from your recipients represents an opportunity to learn something new and improve your future campaigns.

In the email marketing ecosystem, change is the only constant. Technologies, consumer behaviors, the rules of the game—everything can change, and often it does so very rapidly. To maximize your ROI, you must always be ready to adapt, innovate, and evolve your strategies. Adaptability and flexibility are your best allies in this ever-evolving field.

In conclusion, the secret to maximizing ROI in email marketing lies in understanding that email marketing is much more than just a sales tool. It's a complete, sophisticated, and ever-evolving marketing discipline. It's a way to connect with your customers on a personal level, provide them with value, and build lasting relationships. And when done correctly, it can yield a return on investment that far exceeds that of many other forms of marketing.

The hope is that this book has provided you with the knowledge and tools needed to get the most out of your investment in email marketing. And I hope you will continue to experiment, learn, and grow on your journey in email marketing. The future is bright, and the power is in your hands. Happy journey in the world of email marketing!

Final Conclusions

As we embarked on this journey through the world of email marketing, we began by discussing the simple power that resides in your inbox. Now, as we approach the end of our journey, it's time to emphasize that email marketing is not just a powerful tool but also a sophisticated and ever-evolving discipline.

This third book in the series has shed a comprehensive light on the art and science of email marketing, from its fundamentals to the use of advanced strategies. We have delved into creating engaging emails, managing contact lists, measuring campaign performance, various aspects of advanced email marketing strategies, and how these interweave with the realm of social media.

We have explored the beating heart of email marketing: building and managing contact lists. We have learned the importance of constructing healthy and compliant lists, the value of well-defined list segments, and the power of targeted personalizations. We have observed how sound list management practices can lead to substantial improvements in open rates, click-through rates, and conversion rates.

We have analyzed the fundamental KPIs (Key Performance Indicators) of email marketing: open rate, click-through rate, and conversion rate. We have grasped how these metrics can provide valuable insights into the performance of our email campaigns and how to continually enhance our marketing efforts.

Furthermore, we have delved into advanced email marketing strategies such as retargeting, drip campaigns, and upselling, and how these techniques can be employed to maximize the effectiveness of our email campaigns. We have seen how the integration of email and social media can lead to a more comprehensive and cohesive digital marketing strategy.

Finally, we have looked to the future of email marketing and the potential impact of emerging technologies like artificial intelligence. We have seen how AI can bring an unprecedented level of personalization and automation, opening new frontiers for the effectiveness and efficiency of our marketing.

In conclusion, I hope this book has provided you with a clear and comprehensive view of email marketing, its potentials, and its future developments. But most importantly, I hope you can now regard your inbox not just as a simple communication tool but as a powerful marketing lever that, when used correctly, can bring significant value to your business.

Email marketing is a journey, not a destination. And like any journey, success depends not only on the destination but also on the path taken. So, as we close this book, remember that the power of your inbox lies in your hands. Use it wisely, innovate continuously, measure carefully, and optimize proactively. Above all, keep learning, because, as in every form of marketing, the only constant in email marketing is change.

I wish you all the success possible on your journey in email marketing. Remember, the power is in your inbox. Harness it to the fullest.

DigIdentity